STATIONS

—

DOM

FAMILY PUBLICATIONS

OXFORD

ISBN 978-1-871217-88-9

Art credits

Cover: Graduel de Fontevrault, © coll. Bibliothèque francophone de Limoges, France
Page 1: © Bibliothèque municipale d'Arras, Ms 882 (986), fol 95, Cliché IRHT-CNRS
Page 3: © Bibliothèque municipale de Tours, Ms 2104, fol 120, Cliché IRHT-CNRS
Station I: © Bibliothèque municipale de Besançon, Ms 550, fol 87, Cliché IRHT-CNRS
Station II: © Bibliothèque municipale de Tours, Ms 2104, fol 146v, Cliché IRHT-CNRS
Station III: © Bibliothèque Municipale Classée d'Autun, SR 347:
Montée au calvaire, Cliché IRHT-CNRS
Station IV: © BMVR Marseille, Ms 111 : Heures à l'usage de Thérouanne, fol 126,
Initiale D, Montée au calvaire, Cliché IRHT-CNRS
Station V: © Bibliothèque Mazarine, Paris, Ms 976, fol 91v
Station VI: © Bibliothèque Inguimbertine, Carpentras, archives et musées, Ms 61, fol 121v
Station VII: © Collections de la Bibliothèque municipale de Rouen, Leber 142, fol 38,
Photographie Thierry Ascensio-Parvy
Station VIII: © Bibliothèque municipale Livrée Ceccano, Avignon, Ms 121, fol 55v,
Cliché IRHT-CNRS
Station IX: © Bibliothèque municipale de Besançon, Ms 54, fol 14v, Cliché IRHT-CNRS
Station X: © Bibliothèque municipale d'Abbeville, Ms 16, fol 27v, Cliché IRHT-CNRS
Station XI: © Bibliothèque Inguimbertine, Carpentras, archives et musées, Ms 410, fol 18
Station XII: © Bibliothèque municipale d'Aurillac, Ms 2, fol 164
Station XIII: © Bibliothèque municipale Georges-Pompidou de Châlons-en-Champagne,
Ms 336, fol 65v, Cliché IRHT-CNRS
Station XIV: © Bibliothèque municipale de Tours, Ms 217, fol 49, Cliché IRHT-CNRS
Page 32: B. M. V. *Résurrection du Christ* (Ms 118, 100 v°) © Bibliothèque Municipale de
Valenciennes – Ph. F. Leclercq

published by

Family Publications
Denis Riches House, 66 Sandford Lane
Kennington, Oxford, OX1 5RP
www.familypublications.co.uk

printed in Malta by Melita Press
through s|s|media ltd

At the beginning of each station:

℣. *We adore you O Christ and we bless you*
℟. *Because by your holy Cross you have redeemed the world.*

At the conclusion of each station:

I love you Jesus, my Love, above all things,
I repent with my whole heart for having offended you.
Never permit me to separate myself from you again.
Grant that I may love you always
And then do with me what you will.

Between stations, a verse of the Stabat Mater, printed underneath the illustration for each station, may be said or sung.

At the Cross her station keeping,
Stood the mournful Mother weeping
Close to Jesus to the last.

FIRST STATION

JESUS IS CONDEMNED TO DEATH

We adore you O Christ and we bless you
Because by your holy Cross you have redeemed the world.

❧

I am the Way, the Truth and the Life (Jn 14:6)

Jesus stands bound before Pilate. He has been betrayed, arrested and worn down all night by the constant interrogation. Already he has parried a hundred questions as to who he really is, what he has done, and suddenly there is no more need to be silent. "I was born for this, I came into the world for this." Before the man who seeks to overawe him with the threat of death he reveals the real issue for this trial. There is no turning back; here he will take his oath as the witness to the indestructibility of Truth. "I was born for this": the betrayal and the scourges and the mockery and the cross and the resurrection. And Pilate, a pawn in a plan which dwarfs him, passes a sentence of death on the Life of the World.

> O Jesus, I am constantly worrying about what people think, what impression I make on them, how they rate my importance. May I listen instead to your voice so as to be on the side of your truth wherever that causes me to stand, whatever it costs. May I stand before you in the truth of who I am.

❧

I love you Jesus, my Love, above all things ...

Through her heart His sorrow sharing
All His bitter anguish bearing,
Now at length the sword had passed.

Second Station

Jesus Receives the Cross

We adore you O Christ and we bless you
Because by your holy Cross you have redeemed the world.

My yoke is easy and my burden light (Mt 11:30)

Upon the back flayed with scourging he takes the heavy, rough cross and heads out of Jerusalem. The chief priests and elders stand by, watching the scapegoat, driven out with the sins of the nation on His back. It is not yet evident; for to them he is a criminal and a blasphemer and they see the cross as punishment. They do not see that he carries the sins of the world, is taking them away for ever. 'They tie heavy burdens on men's backs but will not lift a finger themselves' he said of them, but in truth no one else could bear such a load as this.

> Dearest Jesus, such is my pride, and sometimes my contrition, that I am occasionally discouraged by the burden of my sins; I don't believe I will ever make progress; I wonder, secretly, if it's worth bothering. When I am weighed down with a sense of sin let me remember that it is not I who carry this burden; you have already borne this weight for me. If I come to you, you will give me rest.

I love you Jesus, my Love, above all things ...

O how sad and sore distressed
Was that Mother highly blessed,
Of the sole begotten One!

THIRD STATION

JESUS FALLS FOR THE FIRST TIME

We adore you O Christ and we bless you
Because by your holy Cross you have redeemed the world.

॰

My soul clings to you, your right hand holds me fast (Ps 62)

Like a toddler learning to walk, he stumbles and totters, seems for a moment as if he will recover balance, only to fall heavily, the cross pinning him to the ground. Here he lies, full stretch on the ground shedding blood, for the second time in twenty-four hours.

In Gethsemane the bystanders slept, now they jeer and shout. Then his prayer was, "Father if it is possible save me." Nevertheless, he drags himself to his feet again, for the Father's will urges him on and an invincible love for those who slept and those who jeer.

If I am honest I sometimes wonder what God is up to. I pray and nothing seems to happen, the pain remains.

Dearest Jesus, teach me by this first fall that I must get up again and again and struggle on with nothing but the assurance of faith that you loved the world so much, you love me so much. Teach me that faith is all about struggling on.

॰

I love you Jesus, my Love, above all things ...

Christ above in torment hangs,
She beneath beholds the pangs
Of her dying glorious Son.

JESUS MEETS HIS MOTHER

We adore you O Christ and we bless you
Because by your holy Cross you have redeemed the world.

Look, he is destined for the fall and
rising of many in Israel (Lk 2:34)

An agony of comfort to see her there. He would have
spared her this; he would not have had her see him so, but
she will not spare herself. Not for all the world would she
see him so, but see him she must. It is as if the pain can be
seen most clearly as it is reflected in each other's eyes. There
its true depths are revealed. No one else can comprehend
what passes in this meeting; it knows no human words.
That is what she said yes to all those years ago, that is what
every mother says yes to, to the mystery of what her child
will become. And see what they are doing to her Son? She
has given him life. Both their pain and their comfort is
mediated through that single thought, and now she must let
him go. In silence she suffers with him.

> O Mary, help me to love with courage, to give my heart
> without fearing the pain that must follow from doing so.

I love you Jesus, my Love, above all things ...

Is there one who would not weep,
Whelmed in miseries so deep
Christ's dear Mother to behold?

THE CROSS IS LAID ON SIMON OF CYRENE

We adore you O Christ and we bless you
Because by your holy Cross you have redeemed the world.

Do you think that I cannot appeal to my Father, and he will at once send me more than twelve legions of angels? But how then should the scriptures be fulfilled? (Mt 26:53-54)

It is becoming more and more painful to watch, each step with the heavy cross seems to bring Jesus nearer to collapse. With who knows what threats and persuasions the soldiers compel a passer-by to help Jesus. This is not out of compassion, rather out of a malicious desire to see that he escapes none of the terrors of Golgotha. He is not to die in custody, he is to be executed. Simon has become the patron saint of those caught up in other people's troubles, those who risk getting involved. He is like the son of whom Jesus speaks in the parable who says "I will not go", and afterwards thinks better of it and goes. He shows us there is a special grace in the tasks from which we recoil.

> Dearest Jesus, may I be generous in seizing chances to be like Simon, to lighten people's loads, to carry the burden of others in prayer. Teach me to be humble enough to recognise my limitations and to accept graciously the help of others, even when I do not understand their motivation.

I love you Jesus, my Love, above all things ...

Can the human heart refrain
From partaking in her pain
In that Mother's pain untold?

VERONICA WIPES THE FACE OF JESUS

We adore you O Christ and we bless you
Because by your holy Cross you have redeemed the world.

❧

You see the crowd pressing all about you yet you say who touched you? (Mk 5:31)

A frightened woman once dared to touch the fringe of his cloak and her haemorrhage was cured. He felt the power go out of him and commended her faith. Now another woman, Veronica, takes a risk and braves the reactions of the soldiers to come forward and wipe his face, to dry the blood from his eyes. Still power comes out of him, a strange power which preserves his image on the cloth as the Man of Sorrows, without beauty, without majesty. The challenge for every would-be disciple is to behold and love him thus, so as to be able to recognise him in his glorious Easter guise. Real faith is to see in my own sufferings the imprint of his own saving Passion.

> Dearest Jesus, teach me that to reflect your face in my living I must first reach out to you in faith, heedless of my safety. I must dare to step out of the crowd.

❧

I love you Jesus, my Love, above all things ...

Bruised, derided, cursed, defiled.
She beheld her tender Child!
All with bloody scourges rent.

SEVENTH STATION

JESUS FALLS FOR THE SECOND TIME

We adore you O Christ and we bless you
Because by your holy Cross you have redeemed the world.

You will arise and have mercy on Zion, for this is the time to have mercy, for your servants love her very stones, are moved with pity even for her dust (Ps 101)

Again he falls and lies inert amid the dust and stones of the road, the Son of God, Eternal Wisdom who was there when the Father made man from the dust of the earth and breathed into his nostrils the breath of life. Now he is a lamentable sight, a mass of bruises and torn flesh, so disfigured he seems barely human. Again the sickening pause; is this the end? Again he drags himself from the ground to continue, for stronger even than the pain is the burning desire to save mankind, creature of dust, and set him on the throne of Heaven, even at the expense of his own life.

> Strong Son of God, Holy and Immortal One, lift me up from the depths of sin and selfishness to share your risen life.

I love you Jesus, my Love, above all things ...

For the sins of His own nation
Saw Him hang in desolation
Till His spirit forth He sent.

THE WOMEN OF JERUSALEM WEEP FOR OUR LORD

We adore you O Christ and we bless you
Because by your holy Cross you have redeemed the world.

Daughters of Jerusalem, weep not for me but for yourselves and for your children (Lk 23:28)

At last there is a group in the crowd who are not hostile, who want to give him their sympathy. These good women have followed him during his days teaching and healing. He must be glad of their concern, but he tells them to save their tears for themselves and their children. For the real Passion of Jesus lies not only in his horrific suffering, but in his confronting the horror of sin and what it does to mankind: the centuries of apostasy and greed, war and hatred and violence. This is what he must bear, and his physical suffering is but an outward sign of how it appals him, and how he will give anything for mankind to be otherwise.

> Dearest Jesus, teach me to bemoan the right things, not just those causes which make me feel moral and courageous, but most of all my sins, by which I may do untold damage to the world and to those I love.

I love you Jesus, my Love, above all things ...

O thou Mother fount of love!
Touch my spirit from above,
Make my heart with thine accord.

JESUS FALLS FOR THE THIRD TIME

We adore you O Christ and we bless you
Because by your holy Cross you have redeemed the world.

❧

For we are brought down low to the dust, our body lies prostrate on the earth, Stand up and come to our help, Redeem us because of your love (Ps 43)

His burden is too much. He collapses beneath it once more, and the pain is like a torrent overwhelming him. It would be good to give in, to let it submerge him, to cease to struggle. But love endures all things, love does not come to an end. He cannot rest, for the burden he bears is the sins of the world and these can never overwhelm Goodness. He will carry this burden of sin to the altar of Calvary and only there lay it down to be consumed in the Father's love.

Sometimes evil does seem overwhelming. It threatens to crush the good. Wherever man feels defeated by it, God is always there in solidarity, urging him to get to his feet, to struggle. Jesus shows us that the human spirit is unquenchable when fired with love for something greater than itself.

O my suffering Jesus, when I feel overwhelmed in my struggles give me the courage to rise and carry my cross onward. Give me sight of your face bearing yours for me.

❧

I love you Jesus, my Love, above all things ...

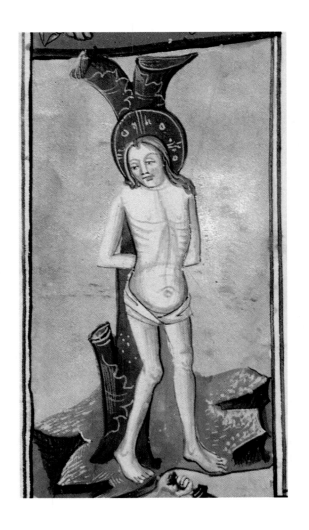

Make me feel as thou hast felt;
Make my soul to glow and melt
With the love of Christ my Lord.

Jesus is stripped of his garments

We adore you O Christ and we bless you
Because by your holy Cross you have redeemed the world.

Behold the bridegroom! (Mt 25:6)

To humiliate him further they strip Jesus's clothes from him, causing him untold agony, for the garments adhere to his wounds. And there he stands, the Second Adam, exposed to the derision of the mob. Mary watches as the soldiers take his clothes and roll dice for them. Seeing the shattered body, how she must long to comfort him.

And he, in this humiliation, thinks of all those who will find their bodies exposed and shamed: the victims of abuse and exploitation. He thinks of them and offers himself as sign of the spousal meaning of the body, and its capacity not for pleasure only, but for making covenant, for giving life. By this degradation he honours and heals all whose bodily dignity is outraged.

> Dearest Jesus, in Baptism I became a new creation and was clothed in your likeness. By your suffering help me to divest myself of all layers with which I have covered my true self, the insecurities, the addictions, the false comforts and pleasure seeking, and to stand exposed to your gaze as the child of God, free from fear or shame.

I love you Jesus, my Love, above all things ...

Holy Mother! Pierce me through;
In my heart each wound renew
Of my Saviour crucified.

JESUS IS NAILED TO THE CROSS

We adore you O Christ and we bless you
Because by your holy Cross you have redeemed the world.

❧

Stretch out your hand over the sea and divide it, that the people of Israel may go on dry ground through the sea
(Ex 14:16)

He stretches his hands wide on the cross and the soldiers drive home the cruel nails. It is at once a gesture of embrace and supplication. He reaches towards the Father and to us in offering, pleading, welcome. With every hammer blow the world's salvation is more secure, more true. For Mary, watching, every stroke wrings her heart. She knows from the Angel, from her very bearing of him, the origins of this Son. She must now watch him tortured to death. With a mother's grief she remembers the baby's hands, tiny and soft, fingers wrapped around hers, and the exquisitely miniature feet of the infant that she would kiss, now bitten by nails.

> Dearest Jesus, your suffering appals and grieves me more than I can say. But in it is my hope for finding forgiveness and atonement. Teach me that when I come to pray, mere gestures and words are not enough, that I must also open my arms to embrace what the Father wills, pain and all, and that I must love everyone; even those who hurt me.

❧

I love you Jesus, my Love, above all things …

Let me share with thee His pain;
Who for all my sins was slain;
Who for me in torments died.

✠

TWELFTH STATION

JESUS DIES ON THE CROSS

We adore you O Christ and we bless you
Because by your holy Cross you have redeemed the world.

❧

He himself bore our sins in his body on the tree (1 Pet 2:24)

The cross is raised and Jesus hangs there in unimaginable pain. Now Jesus has truly accepted our human condition, the sin which destroys man.

Mary can but stand there with him and watch. The hours like years, the words so strange, at once a leave-taking and a thought for her protection, "Woman behold your Son". Then at last the head stoops and falls, as when he used to fall asleep. Now the immense horror of the lance. His heart which once beat with her blood in the depths of her being is pierced and there flows out blood and water, the stuff of dying and of being born.

The lance, and the sword which has pierced Mary's soul, tell us that the human heart must in some way be breached, opened, to allow something even greater to quicken and sustain our existence. The Passion means being emptied out, so that something else may fill that emptiness: the eternal Love of the Father.

O Jesus and Mary, show me how to say 'Let it be done to me what the Father wants', even at the cost of all I hold most dear, until I can say 'It is finished'.

❧

I love you Jesus, my Love, above all things ...

Let me mingle tears with thee,
Mourning Him who mourn'd for me
All the days that I may live.

JESUS IS TAKEN DOWN FROM THE CROSS

We adore you O Christ and we bless you
Because by your holy Cross you have redeemed the world.

❧

My child ... see how worried your father and I have been (Lk 2:48)

With difficulty they take the shattered body of Jesus off the cross and Mary enfolds him in her arms. This is the body she swaddled and nursed, whose childish limbs she bathed and clothed, now livid and cold. This is her son, but he is also the Son of God. This horror is man's redemption, but Mary cannot yet know how. It can hardly be a comfort to Mary to know that this child of hers is the Son of God. It must rather be the most appalling desolation imaginable. Long ago she said yes to the angel who said "He will be great and will be called Son of the Most High." It is impossible to imagine what Mary feels; she has lost her Son, she has lost the Son of God. She lost him once before, but it was not like this, this utter finality. No wonder there are no words; no wonder Mary is silent. It is like a sword opening her heart to new and greater expanses of pain which she did not believe it possible to feel. But she ponders with hope: "Did you not know I must be about my Father's business? Woman ... my hour has not yet come."

> O Mary, comfort of the afflicted, be with me in all my bereavements and teach me to hope in your Son.

❧

I love you Jesus, my Love, above all things ...

Onuerte nos deus saluta
ns noster:

By the Cross with thee to stay;
There with thee to weep and pray,
Is all I ask of thee to give.

FOURTEENTH STATION

JESUS IS LAID IN THE TOMB

We adore you O Christ and we bless you
Because by your holy Cross you have redeemed the world.

O where can I go from your spirit? Where can I flee from your face? If I lie in the grave you are there (Ps 138)

They take the body of Jesus and wrap it hastily for burial before sunset. There is some shred of comfort in this activity; the body remains all that they have of Jesus and to tend it shows the love they feel. In their attachment to it, they express an instinct that life cannot end so, that there must be something else, some other finality for those we love. With this hope, they place him in a borrowed tomb and depart to face the emptiness and silence left by death. Every such scene, every hospital mortuary, graveside and crematorium knows this emptiness, this pain at parting from the body of someone we loved. And the same hope dawns on them, as on his tomb, for by his death Jesus has opened even the depths of the grave to the Spirit of God's love, the Spirit who breathes life. The resurrection was then a mystery beyond the horizon of those who buried Jesus. To us it has been revealed, in us it is already at work through our Baptism; now our true life is hidden with Christ in God. He will not let his beloved know decay.

> Dearest Jesus, hide me in your wounds, let me rest there
> in safety, there forever share your glorious life.

I love you Jesus, my Love, above all things ...

ON THE THIRD DAY HE ROSE AGAIN